GALAXY OF SUPERSTARS

98°	Faith Hill
Ben Affleck	Lauryn Hill
Jennifer Aniston	Jennifer Lopez
Backstreet Boys	Ricky Martin
Brandy	Ewan McGregor
Garth Brooks	Mike Myers
Mariah Carey	'N Sync
Matt Damon	Gwyneth Paltrow
Cameron Diaz	LeAnn Rimes
Leonardo DiCaprio	Adam Sandler
Céline Dion	Will Smith
Sarah Michelle Gellar	Britney Spears
Tom Hanks	Spice Girls
Hanson	Jonathan Taylor Thomas
Jennifer Love Hewitt	Venus Williams

CHELSEA HOUSE PUBLISHERS

GALAXY OF SUPERSTARS

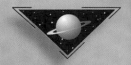

Faith Hill

Bonnie Hinman

CHELSEA HOUSE PUBLISHERS
Philadelphia

Frontis: Seen here in concert in Las Vegas, Faith Hill has struck a delicate balance between a successful music career and an enriching family life.

CHELSEA HOUSE PUBLISHERS

Editor in Chief: Sally Cheney
Associate Editor in Chief: Kim Shinners
Production Manager: Pamela Loos
Art Director: Sara Davis

Produced by
21st Century Publishing and Communications, Inc.
New York, New York
http://www.21cpc.com

The Chelsea House World Wide Web address is
http://www.chelseahouse.com

First Printing

1 3 5 7 9 8 6 4 2

Library of Congress Cataloging-in-Publication Data

Hinman, Bonnie,
    Faith Hill / Bonnie Hinman.
        p. cm. — (Galaxy of superstars)
    Includes bibliographical references and indexes.
    Summary: Examines the private life and professional career of country music star, Faith Hill.
    ISBN 0-7910-6471-9 (alk. paper)
    1. Hill, Faith, 1967–   —Juvenile literature. 2. Country musicians—United States—Biography—Juvenile literature. [1. Hill, Faith, 1967–   .
2. Singers. 3. Country music. 4. Women—Biography.] I. Title. II. Series.

ML3930.H53 H56 2001
782.421642'092—dc21
[B]   2001042088

CONTENTS

CHAPTER 1
OLD TIME TUNES   7

CHAPTER 2
THE GIRL FROM STAR   15

CHAPTER 3
PATIENCE REWARDED   23

CHAPTER 4
SPONTANEOUS COMBUSTION   33

CHAPTER 5
CROSSOVER STAR   41

CHAPTER 6
THE GOOD LIFE   51

CHRONOLOGY   60
ACCOMPLISHMENTS   61
FURTHER READING   62
INDEX   64

1

OLD TIME TUNES

"To me, music has a power all its own. It can bring us together. It can move us. It can heal us. Music can change your life. I know. It changed mine." With these simple, yet powerful, words country music superstar Faith Hill opened her first network television special on Thanksgiving night 2000.

The Palace Auditorium in Auburn Hills, Michigan, sparkled with lights and rang with the cheers of fans as Faith was seen backstage striding toward the stage. Moments before, Faith had spoken from her dressing room to the television audience: "This year has been one of the most unforgettable years of my life. And tonight I get to express my appreciation the best way that I know how—by singing for you."

At the last moment Faith's husband, country music star Tim McGraw, pulled her close for a quick kiss before she burst onto the stage to the enthusiastic screams of her fans. Fittingly, Faith's first number was "This Kiss," her award-winning hit from 1998. Her long blonde hair flew behind her as she belted out the song that had sealed her stardom.

In between numbers, the television special had film clips of Faith talking to her backup singers, playing basketball

---

Faith Hill is one of the most successful crossover recording artists. Her single "Breathe" hit number one on both the pop and country music charts.

with Tim, and just speaking of her experiences. She talked about her eight years of touring and related how lucky she felt to get to do something she loves so much.

Faith sang "Breathe," her most recent hit, as a breeze ruffled her hair and a filmy backdrop swayed behind her. The television cameras showed the delighted faces of Faith's fans as they watched her performance. When she sang "It Matters To Me," the audience joined in.

Faith's duet with husband Tim was especially popular with fans. Tim and Faith slow-danced during part of their romantic duet, "Let's Make Love," and hugged at the end as the audience erupted into applause and cheers.

The grand finale for Faith's Thanksgiving special reflected both the holiday and Faith's spiritual feelings. "There Will Come a Day" is a toe-tapping gospel number and was backed up by a black-robed choir who sang and clapped as Faith sang. The song's verses told of the cruel and sad events that can happen to people. The chorus came back with a strong telling of Faith's own beliefs:

> There's another place where our Father waits
> And every tear He'll wipe away
> The darkness will be gone
> The weak shall be strong
> Hold on to your faith
> There will come a day
> There will come a day.

The spotlight this first television special shone on Faith Hill was a bright one indeed, but her career had brought her to this highlight. Like most artists, she had many years of little or no success. Hard work and talent have brought her up through the ranks of country music and put her right at the top. Her ability to appeal to pop music fans as well as country fans has been a big boost to her success.

But Faith has often found herself at the center of controversy over the difference behind the traditional country music and the new country sound. Critics might ask of her Thanksgiving special—it's glamorous, it's glitzy, but is it country? The joining of country and pop music has been many years in the making. Country music and popular music have coexisted for decades. It would be hard to say for certain which came first.

Country music has its roots in the old British folk songs and fiddle tunes. The songs came to America with British immigrants and quickly began to merge with music brought by other immigrants from countries such as Germany, France, Spain, and Africa. This resulting patch-work of musical styles and tunes made up American folk music.

The violin or fiddle, as it was called by people in rural areas, was the instrument of choice. It was portable and lent itself to all kinds of music. With a fiddle and some floor space, a community could have a barn dance. Life was hard for most early Americans, and they used every opportunity possible to enjoy the simple pleasure of music.

In those early days music was shared in two ways: through sheet music and face to face. Sheet music was available for classical music and music hall songs, but any folk music was strictly passed from person to person. Many of the fiddlers played only by ear, so they learned from each other and from traveling musicians. In most cases, folk music wasn't written down.

By 1920 the world was changing quickly

Early Americans came together at barn dances to enjoy country music. The fiddle was the instrument of choice.

and music was changing with it. Over 7 million homes had phonographs, but the big record companies didn't think that country dwellers would spend their scarce cash for folk music records. Radio was the force that set country music's popularity in motion.

Five years later, relatively inexpensive radios were available, and record sales began to decline. One record cost about $.75, while a battery-powered crystal radio set sold for only $1.00. Record companies looked around for a way to improve sales and happened on folk music, or what was often called old time tunes.

After some early success with the old time tunes, record company scouts set out across the country, particularly the southeast, to find new singers and groups. Record sales began to pick up, but it was still radio that promoted country music. New stations were popping up everywhere. Many of the southern and mid-western stations had what was called a barn dance show. These live radio shows were variety shows with old time music and comedy.

A new radio station signed on in Nashville, Tennessee, on October 5, 1925. WSM probably contributed more to the rise of the country music business than any other single force. George Hay, a newspaper reporter turned radio announcer, was hired as the station director for WSM a few weeks after its start. He was experienced with the old time tunes and soon had a Saturday night barn dance show on WSM.

This fast-paced show featured hoedown bands, comedy acts, and lots of old time songs. Hay gave the bands colorful names like the Dixie Clodhoppers, the Fruit Jar Drinkers, and the Gully Jumpers. He insisted that they dress in overalls and beat-up hats for publicity pictures. This was the show that became the Grand Ole Opry.

George Hay actually named the show by accident. One evening he needed to introduce some of the barn dance musicians who were filling in for a half hour between two other shows. The network show just ending had been one of classical music, so George was inspired to make the transition by announcing, "For the past hour we have been listening to the music taken largely from Grand Opera, but from now on we will present the Grand Ole Opry!" The name stuck when the following Sunday morning the local newspaper referred to the Saturday night show as the "Grand Old Op'ry."

"Country" music was born but it still wasn't called by its familiar name. For many of the early years the old time music came to be known as hillbilly music. The musicians referred to themselves as hillbillies, so that name attached itself to their music. The Grand Ole Opry's popularity grew steadily even during the Great Depression in the 1930s.

Eventually the phrase "country and western" began to be used to describe the music coming out of Nashville. Country music soon split into several different sounds and styles. There was western swing and the singing cowboys of Hollywood movies. Gene Autry and Roy Rogers made their mark in the early singing cowboy movies.

After World War II, rockabilly got its start and was a forerunner of rock and roll music. Elvis Presley started out as a rockabilly singer. In the 1950s, Patsy Cline began a brief but memorable career recording mostly slow mournful ballads. In the 1960s what was called the Nashville sound moved away from the instrumentation of traditional country music and made a step in the direction of pop music.

In the 1970s and 1980s, country music's popularity expanded and the audience broadened as more and more country artists had crossover hits. A crossover hit happens when a song or album climbs high on both the country and pop charts. This brought the first controversy over what is real "country." It's basically the same controversy that artists such as Faith Hill deal with today. The last 20 years have brought dozens of television specials and series featuring country stars each more glamorous and slick than the last. The music generally uses little if

Faith Hill is one of the most popular singers in country music today. However, there has been some controversy over her music because many of her country hits have crossed over to the pop charts.

any fiddles or steel guitars, which are the mainstay of old-fashioned country music.

Is it country music, or has the sound gone "pop"? While the country music of George Strait and Reba McEntire is in Faith Hill's heart and soul, she wants to sing and please her fans at the same time. She'll leave it to someone else to name her sound. When Faith performs, her fans don't care what you call her music, they simply love it.

2

THE GIRL
FROM STAR

Faith Hill was born in Jackson, Mississippi, on September 21, 1967, but her life really began a few days later when she was adopted by Ted and Edna Perry. The Perrys named their baby Audrey Faith and took her home to tiny Star, Mississippi. Two older brothers waited there to meet their baby sister. Wesley was eight and Steve was seven.

The Perrys worked hard to provide for their children. Ted worked in a factory, and sometimes Edna had more than one job to help put food on the table. But as important as food, and clothes, and a bed to sleep in are, they aren't the things that Faith remembers best from her childhood. "God was watching over me and put me in this incredible home where I had a great family life," she recalls. "If you show love to someone, it's amazing what possibilities it gives that person in life. I know how lucky I am."

Early on it became obvious that music would play a role in Faith's life. "My mom will tell you that I was born singing, but the truth is I started when I was three years old." The Perrys went to church every Sunday, and Faith

---

While Faith's music career blossomed in the early 90s, she began singing at age three and she joined the children's choir at her church when she was just seven years old.

joined in the hymn singing with all the energy a three-year-old, who held the hymnal upside-down, could muster.

At home Faith followed her big brothers around, getting her share of scrapes and bruises. It was a great life for a lively child like Faith. Her mother dressed her in frilly dresses on Sunday but let her be a tomboy the rest of the time. She once described herself: "I'm a tough girl, raised with two brothers. You better believe I know how to take care of myself."

Faith joined the children's choir at her church when she was seven. That same year she had her first public performance when she sang at a 4-H mother-daughter luncheon. Sometimes when the family had company, Faith's mother would give her a quarter to sing for the guests. Singing at a family reunion might be worth 50 cents. She sang Sunday School songs like "Jesus Loves Me" and popular songs of the time like "Delta Dawn." She loved to perform and the pay, when Mom offered it, wasn't bad either.

When Faith was in elementary school, she found out that her father couldn't read. Ted Perry had 12 brothers and sisters and left school in the fourth grade to work and help support the family. Faith didn't realize the limits this placed on her father until she was an adult. She only knew that her father, although loving in every way, didn't help with homework or read stories to his children.

The first music Faith came to love besides church music was that of Elvis Presley. The first album she ever owned was one of his, and she saw him in concert in 1975. Although Elvis was past his prime by that time, his music, with its strong connections to gospel and country,

In high school, Faith idolized country superstar Reba McEntire. She knew she wanted to be a singer at an early age.

appealed greatly to Faith. Whatever his short-comings, Elvis sang with great passion and purpose, which were qualities that Faith had, too.

By the time Faith reached high school she idolized country singer Reba McEntire, but had added many other activities to her interest in music. She was a cheerleader, played sports, and was class president her junior year. A life-long friend, Kathy Jones, said, "Faith never did anything halfway. In cheerleading she didn't just chant, she screamed."

Even with the whirlwind of activities that high school brought, music was still at the heart of Faith's life. "I was 14 when I consciously decided to become a singer," Faith recalls. She sang at church and with the youth choir at other churches. Later she sang with a country band at rodeos, county fairs, and private parties.

One of her more memorable gigs from those days was as the entertainment at a tobacco spit in Raleigh, Mississippi. The spitters aimed for spittoons at the far end of the stage, competing to see who could spit tobacco juice the farthest. The stage had to be toweled off before Faith could perform.

Faith graduated from McLaurin High School in 1986 and attended Hinds Community College in Raymond, Mississippi, that fall. She wanted to get an education because her parents had taught her how important that was, but Nashville called and finally Faith had to answer. She couldn't concentrate on books when all she wanted to do was sing. After one semester of college she loaded up her car and went to Nashville.

Faith's parents may have been worried about their 19-year-old daughter moving to a city to live alone, but they helped her in every way. One of Faith's first jobs in Nashville was at the Fan Fair, a yearly festival that gives country music fans the chance to meet their idols. There are autograph parties, fan-club get-togethers, and concerts. Faith sold T-shirts during the fair and got her first taste of Nashville excitement.

It was a brief but thrilling job. Faith went on to other jobs, one of them a stint working for Reba McEntire's fan club. Since Reba was one of Faith's idols, it was great fun to package the merchandise sold through the fan club. Later Faith admitted to some other feelings about her job. "I was so sick of Reba. I love her so much, but after eight hours a day of Reba shirts and pajamas, clocks and watches, necklaces and key chains and hat pins . . . oh, my Lord!"

Reba remembers her young worker, "Faith was a bright, spunky, feisty girl—real sweet and open, but a little mischievous. She reminded me a lot of myself. When she got nervous or a little flustered, her neck would break out in a rash."

Faith wanted to get a job working for a music business. She had several unsuccessful interviews before she realized that perhaps she was being a little too open about her music ambitions. The companies wanted loyal employees and weren't interested in young singers hoping to make their mark in the music business. On the next interview she kept quiet about her dreams and was hired as a receptionist for Gary Morris Music.

Faith watched and listened and learned about the music business while she answered phones and directed visitors. She later said that it was frustrating because everything was happening around her, but she was getting nowhere with her own music.

Faith's personal life moved faster. She met a music publishing executive named Daniel Hill. They dated for over a year and married on July 23, 1988. Faith was 20 when she married, and later said that she was too young. In spite of difficulties, Faith had been raised to believe that marriage was for keeps, so the couple tried hard to make their partnership work.

Eventually Faith's music career took a few

The Grand Ole Opry is the legendary country music concert hall in Nashville, Tennessee. As a teenager, Faith dreamed of singing there one day.

small steps forward. Faith has said that as a teenager she expected to "get on the Grand Ole Opry stage, start singing, and be on a bus traveling the next day." As with most successful performers, it took several years for Faith to get her career going.

A writer for Gary Morris Music, David Chase, overheard Faith singing one afternoon when she thought she was alone in the office. He asked her to do a demo of a song called, "It Scares Me." A couple of weeks later David played the demo for his boss, Gary Morris. Gary told Faith to get out from behind her desk and get to work. It was just the encouragement Faith needed, and her career began a slow takeoff from there.

3

PATIENCE REWARDED

Faith had her foot in the door but the struggle to get noticed was far from over. She went to the Nashville clubs several nights a week, considering it a kind of training ground as she learned to judge a good song from a great one. She met singer Gary Burr, who asked her to sing backup for him. Gary had regular gigs at a popular club called the Bluebird Café. Faith gladly played second fiddle to Gary as he taught her stage presence, harmony, and writing.

Faith's breakthrough came when a Warner Brothers Records executive, Martha Sharp, heard her at the Bluebird in the summer of 1991. Nothing happened at the time, but a couple of months later Faith and Martha met at a publishing company event. Martha asked if Faith was pursuing a solo career. Faith responded that she and Gary had put together a demo tape in Gary's living room. Martha listened to the demo, liked what she heard, and took the first steps toward getting a contract for Faith.

Martha made a couple of important contacts for Faith during this time. She talked with Scott Hendricks, a music producer, who worked with many country stars; Martha

---

Faith moved to Nashville to pursue her singing career in 1986 at the age of 19. Faith's big break came when a writer for Gary Morris Music overheard her singing and asked her to record a demo.

also introduced Faith to Gary Borman, an agent who managed several stars.

Even with a contract in hand, success wasn't guaranteed for Faith. It was many months before she recorded her first song. In the meantime, her personal life was like a roller-coaster ride. Faith began the search for her biological mother a couple of years after moving to Nashville. Her family always supported her in her search; her brother Wesley even did some of the footwork. Faith described the quest as "a lot of searching and a lot of digging. I have to believe that it was meant to happen. Because I would never have found her if it were not for some remarkable coincidences."

At last Faith discovered her birth mother's whereabouts, and a meeting was arranged. Of that meeting Faith said, "I found out that she is a painter, an artist, and she has an incredible sense of style. She's very tall. She's a sweet, sweet woman."

Faith found out that her mother was pregnant but not married and evidently felt she could not keep Faith under those circumstances. Later she married Faith's father, who subsequently died in an accident. Faith has one biological brother whom she met several years ago.

"I have no ill feelings," Faith said in an interview. "At least she gave me a chance to be placed in such a loving family. I found out my grandmother and her sister were musical and sang in the church choir."

As wonderful as the successful end to Faith's search was, there was turmoil in her life too. Her marriage to Daniel Hill was breaking up. Faith hasn't had much to say about her ex-husband and their problems. She usually just says that she was too young to marry.

Daniel Hill has said that the search for Faith's mother played a part in their breakup. "That search consumed much of her energy. Meeting her birth mother was the most profound life-altering experience for her. After that, her world turned upside down. I was part of her old world, and she had to let that world go. But there is no bitterness. I'm proud of her success."

In spite of Faith's distractions, she did try hard to make her marriage work. "Being brought up in a very perfect world, when you get married, you stay married. That didn't happen to me." Telling her parents about the impending divorce was probably the hardest part for Faith. The divorce was final in 1994. But before her divorce, Faith's career went into high gear, and she was heading down the road to success.

In November 1992, Faith made her first television appearance on *Nashville Now*. The following March, she sang in the Grand Ole Opry auditorium for the first time. Singing at the Opry is every aspiring country singer's dream, and Faith was no exception. "I was just numb. And I was out there for two songs, walked off the stage, and I swear, I can't tell you anything about it! Except I saw "WSM Grand Ole Opry," you know, on the microphone there, that's all I can remember! I was so nervous!"

Faith recorded her first album that spring of 1993. She had her chance, but with it came a lot of pressure. The album had to be top-notch, Faith had to promote it tirelessly, and the radio stations had to play it. A successful career is almost always launched with hard work and a little luck, and it was the same for

Faith Hill made her first television appearance on *Nashville Now* in 1992. Her dream of appearing at the Grand Ole Opry came true when she performed there for the first time in March 1993.

Faith. *Take Me as I Am* debuted in the fall of 1993. It didn't immediately shoot to the top of the charts, but it made a good showing, particularly for a first album.

A single from the album was released around the same time as the album came out. "Wild One" turned out to provide the first real buzz about Faith. It climbed steadily on the charts until it was number one on *Billboard* magazine's country singles chart on January 1, 1994. "Wild One" perched at the top of the chart for four weeks. The four-week stay was a record-breaker, since a debut single by a female artist hadn't stayed number one for so long since 1964. Connie Smith was the singer then, and "Once a Day" was the song.

Faith described the first time she heard "Wild One" on the car radio one afternoon in Nashville. "It was incredible! I just cried, screamed and cried and screamed and cried!" Faith had reason to be crying and screaming that fall and winter. Warner Brothers released another single from her album, "Piece of My Heart," which hit number one in April 1994. It was a Faith Hill version of the rock classic by Janis Joplin.

Suddenly Faith found herself in demand. She appeared on many television shows, including *Today* and *Late Night with David Letterman*. Warner Brothers and Faith's manager, Gary Borman, carefully coordinated the appearances to create maximum interest in Faith's album and singles.

"With Faith, we had so much to work with," said Borman. "She's a great person, a genuine person who's down to earth. She's very attractive and on top of that, a great singer. We wanted people to realize that she's not just a new artist, and she's not just a pretty face."

At last it was time to jump on the bus and start the touring that Faith had dreamed of in her teenage years. She was asked to open for Reba McEntire. The opening act performs first in a concert and is usually a rising star or trying to become one. It's not an easy gig, as sometimes the audience really only wants to see the headliner, but it's a necessary step for a new artist to take.

"It was very intimidating and scary," Faith

said of opening for Reba. "All the words you can imagine, pile them into one little bowl and it was that. At the same time I had to be confident. I was given a great opportunity and I didn't want to blow it."

Faith didn't "blow it" and continued to tour throughout the spring and summer of 1994, opening for such acts as Brooks & Dunn, John Michael Montgomery, and Alan Jackson. It was an exhausting schedule, even for a young, energetic performer like Faith. "When I'm [home] in town for a day or so, it's just to get my stuff together around the house. I wash my clothes; I like to watch movies, piddle around my house, go through my closets and drawers."

Faith also liked to cook in her limited free time. She thought lasagna was probably her best dish but said that whatever she was cooking usually required a call to her mom to ask, "Okay, how much of that do I put in?"

Faith took time out from touring and appearances to collect an important award. The Academy of Country Music named her Top New Female Vocalist in May 1994. At that time she already had two number-one singles from an album that had been out less than six months. She had joined an elite club, but there was no guarantee of lasting success.

Interviews and concerts filled Faith's days. She was either talking or singing every waking hour that summer and fall. In the midst of the thrill of finally being noticed, there was a problem. Something was wrong with Faith's throat. Doctors diagnosed a burst blood vessel. It wasn't that difficult to repair, but no singer wants to hear the words, "throat surgery."

"I just didn't get it," Faith said later. "I thought there was no way that all that talking

The Academy of Country Music named Faith Hill the Top New Female Vocalist in 1994. She suddenly found herself in great demand.

could hurt me. Heck, I've talked all my life, and it's never affected me. But the stress of traveling and singing constantly, I had this blood vessel in my throat that just burst."

Faith's surgery went smoothly, and after a few months off she resumed singing with a new respect for her voice and the need to take care of it. The break had given her time to look for new songs for her next album and reflect on the direction of her life and career.

Faith's single, "Wild One," reached number one on *Billboard* magazine's country singles chart on January 1, 1994. This was followed by the release of another number one single in April, "Piece of My Heart."

Her personal life took on new direction during her recovery. She had been dating Scott Hendricks, who produced her album. With Faith on the road and Scott back in the studio in Nashville, the couple didn't see as much of each other as they would have liked. Even so, their relationship was serious, and on Valentine's Day 1995 Scott asked Faith to marry him. She said 'yes,' but they didn't set a date for the wedding. The couple had a bigger project underway. As soon as Faith's throat was healed, she would be back in the studio recording her second album.

Recording a second album can be challenging for an artist. The pressure is on—particularly if the first release was a huge success. Faith had the usual fears of being able to live up to big expectations, but she also had to worry about her voice. Would it be the same after surgery? Only the first day back in the studio would answer that question.

4

SPONTANEOUS COMBUSTION

F aith's doctor assured her that her voice would be fine, but she was worried when the time came to record her second album, *It Matters to Me.* She had been practicing vocal exercises, but the true test would come when she was standing in front of the microphone.

To her great relief, the sound came out as before. Perhaps it was even better. The unexpected vacation after her surgery had given Scott and Faith time to sift through hundreds of songs to find just the right 10 for the album. "We put a lot of heart, and soul, and passion into finding each one of the songs that are on the record," Faith has said.

The songs showed the many different sides of Faith's talent. "Let's Go to Vegas" was a romantic and upbeat charmer while "A Man's Home Is His Castle" was a dark tale of abuse. Most of the other numbers were serious stories of life and love's ups and downs.

The exception was the final cut on the album. "Keep Walkin' On" was a gospel song. "I just wanted the listener to be left with the positive message that this is what I believe and this is how I keep going every day," Faith said of her decision to include the song.

When Faith embarked on the Spontaneous Combustion Tour in March 1996, she had no idea how it would change her life. Headlining the tour was country star Tim McGraw, the man who would later become Faith's partner in life.

Faith was joined by singer Shelby Lynne on "Keep Walkin' On." The pair sang the song for the 1995 Country Music Association Awards, and it was a big hit.

It Matters to Me was released in early fall of 1995. Faith took to the road again, touring with Alan Jackson. She was asked in an interview with *Music City News* how she felt about performing live now that she was no longer a beginner. "I just feel a lot more comfortable and confident in my performing abilities on stage, and how I guide a show and carry myself."

Faith's fans didn't desert her with her sophomore album. Sales climbed steadily, and three songs released as singles made it to the top five on the *Billboard* chart. The title track, "It Matters to Me," was the second single to be released and shot to the top of the charts. It hung on to number one for three weeks in January 1996.

The tour that changed Faith's life got underway on March 14, 1996, in West Virginia. The Spontaneous Combustion Tour turned out to be appropriately named. Officially, Tim McGraw was the headliner, and Faith was the opener. But in many respects it was a joint tour.

Tim and Faith had met a couple of times before but didn't really know each other. That soon changed as the couple spent more and more time together off stage. They found that they had a lot in common beyond their love of country music. They both felt that their careers were important but both also wanted a family.

Tim had also grown up in a small town, although his childhood wasn't as happy as Faith's. Tim found out at age 11 that the man he had known as his father was, in fact, a stepfather. Horace Smith had married Tim's

Sparks flew between Faith and country superstar Tim McGraw on their Spontaneous Combustion Tour in 1996. Later that year, Tim proposed to Faith.

mother when Tim was a baby. Tim actually was the son of Tug McGraw, a successful major league baseball player. Tim's mother, Betty Trimble, had known Tug McGraw before he was famous.

Tim eventually got to meet his biological father, just as Faith had met her mother. This shared experience helped build a bond between the two singers. The relationship wasn't entirely a smooth road to happiness. For one thing, each singer didn't think the other was interested. "Whenever I could, I would try to bump into him," Faith recalled later. "I was so attracted to him, and though I didn't know it at the time, he was feeling the same exact thing!"

"I thought she was way out of my league," Tim said. Finally he asked her to meet him after a show one night. "I couldn't stand it anymore." He "planted a big old kiss on her."

"I was shocked, but it was nice," Faith said. Now that the ball was rolling on their romance, there were a few things to straighten out. Faith was still engaged to Scott Hendricks, who was working back in Nashville while Faith was on tour. "It obviously wasn't a rock-solid situation or it wouldn't have ended. Tim is not the reason I left. But I wasn't about to let Tim slip through my hands."

Meanwhile, there were a few other events taking place in Faith's career. In May 1996, Faith, along with Warner Brothers Records and Time Warner, established the Faith Hill Family Literacy Project. This project was started as a tribute to Faith's father and creates awareness of the problem of illiteracy in the United States.

Faith began using her position as a celebrity to encourage the public to get involved in the fight against illiteracy. The project encourages adults to read to children, donate extra books to schools or libraries, and to volunteer to tutor in local literacy programs. "When I was a child," said Faith, "I loved to read. It opened my eyes to the world and helped me realize my dream of becoming a country singer."

Faith received a huge honor on August 4, 1996, when she was asked to perform at the closing ceremonies of the Summer Olympic Games in Atlanta, Georgia. Along with artists such as Stevie Wonder, Gloria Estefan, and the Pointer Sisters, she performed for a worldwide television audience of over 3 billion people.

Late summer found Tim and Faith still touring and on the verge of a romantic commitment. Tim recalls a Jeep ride in Pennsylvania and the conversation they had as a turning point in their relationship. "It was a conversation about our future. That was the point where we realized we wanted to be together for the rest of our lives."

"I saw that we had some of the same goals in life," said Faith. "Our careers were important, but we wanted a family. We wanted that stability."

The couple was still on tour in Montana when Tim popped the big question right before he went on stage for his part of the concert. Faith didn't answer him then, but when he came off stage later, her answer was scrawled on the mirror in his dressing room. Of course the answer was a heartfelt 'yes.'

Faith and Tim may have felt that they were alone in their own little world, but the fans were noticing that something was going on between the two stars. The duo sang a couple of songs together during the show, and the large video screens in the concert halls made some suspect that more than a purely professional relationship existed between Faith and Tim as they danced and sang to each other onstage. Rumors flew, and even Tim's mother was questioned.

"They're dating," Betty Trimble told *Country Weekly* magazine, "but it's nothing beyond that right now. I know I wouldn't mind if it went further because I think they make each other happy and I really like Faith."

Wedding plans were made with much secrecy. One of the tour dates was in northeast Louisiana, where Tim grew up. This was the third year that Tim had done a benefit concert for his old

Faith Hill and Tim McGraw were married on October 6, 1996. Soon, the couple would become parents to Gracie Katherine McGraw and Maggie Elizabeth McGraw.

community. Known as "Swampstock," the annual concerts had raised thousands of dollars for local baseball fields and scholarships. Tim's aunt lived in Rayville, and it was in her backyard that the wedding took place.

The guests arrived for what they thought was a brunch before a charity softball game on October 6, 1996. They were surprised but pleased to find that a wedding was about to start. The ceremony took place under an oak tree in the yard. Faith wore a white dress and veil while Tim stuck to blue jeans and a long black jacket. The family members and close friends who attended were sworn to secrecy until that evening at the concert when Tim introduced his bride to the audience.

The Spontaneous Combustion Tour came to an end with 1996, and the newlyweds sang in the New Year at the Nashville Arena. They must have been looking forward to 1997 with happy expectations especially since they knew that they would become parents by midyear.

The new year brought a welcome break from touring and recording for Faith. Some of the pressure was off, but there was still performing to be done. During the tour, Faith had often joined Tim on a song called "It's Your Love." It hadn't been recorded yet, but Tim had plans to include it on his next album. When he got down to the business of recording his fourth album, *Everywhere*, he asked Faith to sing with him on "It's Your Love."

Faith was pleased to sing the supporting vocals. By the time the recording got underway, Faith was seven months pregnant, and being in the studio required all the energy she could gather. In spite of the extra effort required, she pulled it off beautifully. Tim later said of himself and the producers in the studio, "Afterwards, we all looked at each other and just felt like we had some magic there."

At the 1997 Academy of Country Music Awards held in May, Tim and Faith sang "It's Your Love" to an enthusiastic audience of their peers. That response was just a preview of the overwhelming popularity that the song would have when it was released as a single.

Faith and Tim's careers were soaring, but now it was time to turn their attention to their private lives. They were about to become parents.

5

CROSSOVER STAR

Faith and Tim's daughter, Gracie Katherine McGraw, was born on May 5, 1997, at 8:12 A.M. She was born over three weeks early and weighed only 4 pounds and 14 ounces. Even so, she was healthy and went home right on schedule with her mother.

The new parents settled into the exhausting routine of caring for a new baby. Faith took time off from touring, and Tim adjusted his schedule so he could spend more time at home with Faith and Gracie. The parents shared the child-care duties when Tim was at home, and sometimes Faith took Gracie to see Tim while he was touring.

Gracie took to touring in a way that might be expected of a Faith Hill/Tim McGraw offspring. She even slept through the night the first time on the tour bus. Faith said, "It would be a lot different if she didn't do well on the road. It would change everything."

At home the couple adjusted as all new parents do—with lots of trial and error. According to Faith, "Tim and I made this agreement. I said, 'Honey, I'm going to learn to put on my makeup as quick as you can feed her cereal.

Faith continued to produce albums and tour while starting her family. Here she is pictured with daughter Gracie at a concert in Nebraska while almost 9 months pregnant with her second child, Maggie.

When you finish the cereal, I'll take her and you can go jump in the shower.' We've got this down to a science, really."

In September of that year Tim and Faith won the Vocal Event of the Year award from the Country Music Association for "It's Your Love." Their popular duet gathered even more honors the following spring when they were nominated for awards in four categories by the Academy of Country Music. When the presentation ceremony was over, Faith and Tim had collected awards for Single of the Year, Video of the Year, Vocal Event of the Year, and Song of the Year. It was a clean sweep for the sweethearts of country music.

Meanwhile there was still work to be done in the recording studio. Faith took advantage of time off from touring to work on her next album, which would be called *Faith*. She took her time selecting the songs to be included. With the pressure of her second album behind her, Faith said, "I didn't know what I wanted to do. All I know is I wanted to make a great record."

It turned out to be a difficult process. Faith had matured and wanted her next album to reflect that musically. "The process was about discovering new places in myself, and that is hard, hard work." Faith used two producers, which in itself was unusual. She worked closely with each one to get the desired result. Afterward she said of *Faith*, "It sort of congealed, like a salad that's been in the refrigerator for a long time. It just happened . . . a beautiful salad; this wonderful fruit. And I'm so proud of it; I could not have done a better record, and I can't wait to play it live."

But Faith experienced some frustration with her voice while working on the album. She called her friend, singer Amy Grant, to say, "Amy, this is really frustrating. My voice is different." Her friend told her not to pressure herself and let the hormones present after the birth of Gracie run their course. Eventually, Faith said she thought she was, "singing better than I've ever sung." Motherhood had agreed with her musically as well as personally.

Tim and Faith had another production underway that had nothing to do with music. Less than a year after Gracie's birth, Faith was pregnant again. The McGraws had often spoke of wanting several children, so this came as no surprise—except for the timing. Even though she was pregnant, Faith plunged back into touring to promote *Faith*, which was released in the spring of 1998.

In March 1998 Faith and Tim joined George Strait's tour, which was scheduled to run through June. It was a group tour with fans getting a taste of several different big artists. Gracie went on tour full-time with her parents for the first time. Faith credited Gracie for helping her mom take the ups and downs of touring in stride. "It's easier now," Faith said of being in the limelight. "Once you have a child, things just start to click. I think the reason for that is Gracie is the absolute focal point of my life, and Tim's life. And all the other little things, I really don't care about anymore. I don't worry about it so much."

The release of "This Kiss" from the third album as a single indicated a big change in Faith's career. This irresistibly lively song about the power of a kiss shot to the top of country charts and soon began showing up on the pop charts as well. By fall of 1998 "This Kiss" was in the top five on those pop charts. Faith had officially "crossed over" to pop music.

Faith said of the song, "It changed my life. It's amazing that a song can do that. It's the true power of music. It was one of those rare songs that come along in a career."

This time Faith worked right up until it was time for her second child to be born. During the summer, she and Tim had done the state fair and music festival circuit. And then on August 12, 1998, they were delighted to welcome Maggie Elizabeth McGraw.

Faith's career was red-hot with the success of "This Kiss," so she didn't take much time off after Maggie's birth. Instead she gave interviews, made appearances, and began the long process of producing a fourth album.

Faith was on a year-long high in 1999. In the spring, Faith celebrated her success with an appearance on cable television's 1999 VH1 *Divas Live*. With the invitation to appear on this show, she was being honored as more than a country singer. Tina Turner, Cher, Whitney Houston, and Brandy were some of the artists who shared the stage with her. Faith Hill had joined the big time.

Faith's wide appeal led to other opportunities. Faith was asked to be a spokesperson for Cover Girl Cosmetics. "It was just one of those things that fell from the sky," Faith said of her selection. "One day I got a phone call and the next day I'm in New York and I'm signed to Cover Girl. It was a shock." The contract included magazine ads and television commercials.

Faith Hill appeared on the 1999 *Divas Live* to celebrate her success as an artist. She was honored to be in the company of singing legends Tina Turner, Cher, and Whitney Houston.

Faith had never modeled before, but she had plenty of experience with photo shoots for albums and videos. She felt like she was a good choice for Cover Girl because the company emphasizes the same natural approach to makeup that she does. "I think what attracted them to me was that I'm a working mom, I have a career, and I try to look nice, stay in shape, and be healthy," Faith said of her selection by Cover Girl. "All those things are important. It's not really a glamour thing. It's beauty from the inside out."

Despite her growing list of commitments, Faith decided to go on tour. Faith's first head-lining tour, called the "This Kiss," was a mile-stone for her. She was proud that this time she was in charge. "I've always been the opening act and used other people's equipment. But this time everything is mine. The stage, the backdrops, the way the lights run, the sound—everything. There's even a grand piano onstage. It's everything I wanted. I pay for it every night and it's mine," she said.

Of course the first tour with two little girls was a logistics challenge. When they flew, the family traveled with a giant hockey bag stuffed with toys, two diaper bags, snacks, two car seats, and favorite blankets. Faith preferred to travel by bus, which allowed a lot more freedom and comfort for all of them. The girls were nine months old and two years old, and even with a full-time nanny it was an exhausting gig. "I won't lie: it's a lot of work, and I'm tired. Having two little girls so close in age is almost like having twins. But we learned how to pack and get around and do what we have to do. It's amazing what you can wake up every morning and accomplish as long as you're happy."

Of course part of that happiness was see-ing Tim every few days. He was on the road, too, but they vowed never to spend more than three days apart. So they saw quite a bit of each other. It was a scheduling nightmare for their management companies, but it was a system that worked for the McGraw family.

"We're together most of the time," Faith said. "We hate to be apart. And Gracie is at the age where she's always asking for her dad now. She's Daddy's girl."

There were occasional breaks in the tour, and one such break found the McGraws at the Academy of Country Music awards show. After such a big year with her third album and crossover hit, "This Kiss," it was no surprise to anyone but Faith that she walked away with five awards. "It was unbelievable," Faith said of her win. "It was almost surreal. The whole evening was a bit overwhelming."

Faith also related that the comedown from star to mom was quick in coming after the show. "When we went back to the hotel, Maggie and Gracc woke up. Then we were back to reality! We had to work really hard for another hour and a half to get those two girls back down to sleep. It brings you back down to earth quickly."

The tour had another goal besides that of promoting Faith's album and singles. Faith's Family Literacy Project joined forces with America's Promise, which was led by General Colin Powell, in collecting new and slightly used books at her concerts. Collection centers were set up outside each show's entrance so fans could bring books, which were later distributed in the local community. Elementary schools, hospitals, day-care centers, and battered women/children's shelters received over 25,000 books over the course of the tour.

Cracker Barrel Old Country Stores, which were a sponsor of Faith's tour, collected over a million additional books in their 400-plus locations around the country. Faith's fans have made a difference in the fight against illiteracy.

Her 1998 groundbreaking album, *This Kiss* earned Faith five Academy of Country Music Awards, while her crossover single "This Kiss" placed her at the top of both the pop and country music worlds.

As the "This Kiss" tour finished up, Faith couldn't look forward to a much-deserved rest. Her fourth album, *Breathe,* wasn't finished, and she had only six weeks to do the job.

6

THE GOOD LIFE

With Faith's crossover to pop, her fourth album had a new audience to please. Faith has always insisted that she sings the songs that have meaning to her rather than any particular audience, but there was no doubt that a new group of fans would be considering whether or not to buy her latest album.

Planned or not, *Breathe* did appeal to a wide audience with its mixture of different musical styles. It contained country, pop, gospel, and rhythm and blues songs. "I reached a certain place last year, a certain level of success, and now its time to go to another place," Faith said. "In order to succeed you can't be afraid to fail. Yes, I decided to take some chances here musically—as an artist, that is who I am," Faith said of *Breathe*. "I've always tried to achieve and to do better."

Breathe was released in November 1999 and quickly proved that Faith's instincts about what her fans would like were right on target. The album sold 3 million copies in the first four months. The title track was released as a single, and it was Faith's first single to hit number one on both the pop and country charts.

Another single to make a big splash was "Let's Make

Faith's career was flying high with the release of her fourth album, *Breathe*. The album sold three million copies in the first four months of its release.

Love." Tim and Faith recorded this as a duet and also shot a video. It was a romantic testimony to their love for each other.

The year 2000 got off to a big start when Faith sang the national anthem at Super Bowl XXXIV in January. Over a billion people watched on television as Faith performed. "This is a career highlight for me," Faith said before the game. "I have had the opportunity to sing the national anthem for a couple of playoff games but I never thought about making it to the 'big' game." She also assured a reporter that she wouldn't be lip-syncing.

In March 2000 Faith showed her professionalism when she performed at the Academy Awards even though she was given less than 48 hours to get to Hollywood, rehearse, and perform. Whitney Houston had been scheduled to sing but at the last minute was unable to perform. Lili Fini Zanuck, the producer of the Academy Awards show, called on Faith to fill in for Whitney. "When we called her at the last minute and asked her to rescue the show, Faith immediately said yes and got on a plane."

Burt Bacharach, who arranged the show's music, was also impressed with Faith's cool delivery under pressure. "She pulled it off flawlessly with two rehearsals. She's the real thing. She's just totally musical."

Faith's next big event was VH1 *Divas 2000: A Tribute to Diana Ross*, which was televised on April 11. Of course Faith was a veteran of the 1999 *Divas* special, so this appearance was planned well in advance. She sang "Breathe" and "Love Child," which she called one of her favorite Supremes' songs.

June 2000 was jam-packed with exciting events for Faith and Tim. He was named Father

Faith Hill performed the national anthem at the Super Bowl in January 2000. A few months later, she performed at the Academy Awards.

of the Year by the National Fatherhood Initiative, and the couple attended the awards ceremony in Washington, DC, on June 2. In an interview after the ceremony, Tim said that finding Faith had been a turning point in a previously wild life and that she and his daughters give his life focus.

After receiving such an honor, the next night was just as exciting but much less pleasant for Tim and Faith. They were in Buffalo, New York, where Tim was performing in the George Strait Country Music Festival. Tim's friend, singer Kenny Chesney, had just performed his set and was in the parking lot, which was being patrolled by a deputy on horseback. Kenny asked if he could sit on the horse, which the deputy allowed. Apparently Kenny decided to go for a ride and refused to obey orders to stop. Two deputies caught the horse and tried to remove Kenny.

Tim came on the scene about this time, saw his friend being pulled off the horse, and ran to the rescue. He pushed one of the deputies and a scuffle began. In the end Kenny and Tim were arrested and detained for several hours. Felony charges of assaulting an officer were originally filed against Tim but later reduced to disorderly conduct. "That story got blown way out of proportion," Faith said. "Tim was coming to the defense of a friend."

By the following weekend the couple could laugh about the incident and even put a little extra pizzazz into the final show of the George Strait Festival. Fans in Houston roared when Faith, dressed as a police officer, walked onto the stage while Tim was singing "I Like It, I Love It." Faith proceeded to handcuff her husband and lead him off the stage.

Tim and Faith provided excitement for a special group of youngsters in June. Residents of Big Oak Ranch, a facility for disadvantaged children, traveled to Nashville to present a humanitarian award at the TNN Music Awards. The young people met Faith and Tim while they were in Nashville. Keith Denton, Big Oak Ranch's director of development, spoke for the children, "Meeting Tim McGraw and Faith Hill was extraordinary. They radiate all the glamour of show business but remain such nice and sincere people."

The fun for the children wasn't just in meeting Faith and Tim. The couple later donated 125 tickets so their young fans could attend the McGraws' show in Birmingham, Alabama.

On July 12, Faith and Tim kicked off the Soul2Soul Tour 2000. This time Faith was headlining with Tim instead of being the opening act. They each sang a set of songs and then performed together to the delight of their audience. It probably seemed like it would require magic to take such a big show on the road. With 96 crew members and musicians, plus Faith, Tim, and their daughters traveling from city to city in nine buses for weeks on end, the organizers had a huge job. Ten tractor-trailer rigs hauled a custom 448-square-foot stage with four elevators, 176 moving lights, 620 feet of trussing, and 104 speaker cabinets. Meals had to be catered and hotel rooms reserved.

At least scheduling was easier since Faith and Tim didn't have to travel from separate concert halls to spend time together. In fact the whole McGraw family was happily settled into their leased, custom-built tour bus.

Gracie was three years old and Maggie turned two during the tour. The bus was small but held all the necessities for a home away from the girls' Tennessee home. The bus housed some familiar furnishings from home and lots of toys. The girls' playroom moved from bus to hotel to backstage, but it always had certain books, stuffed monkeys, a tea set, and other favorite toys.

On a typical performance night, Tim, Gracie, and Maggie walked with Faith to the ramp leading up to that night's stage. They kissed her, and out she went to face the thousands of fans cheering for her. Tim waited his turn to perform while Maggie and Gracie went back to their playroom. Later their nanny would put them to bed in the bus or hotel.

Faith tried hard to keep a routine in place for her daughters, and it seemed to work. "Maggie wakes up every single morning at 5:00 Central," Faith told *People* magazine in August 2000, "We're all trying to wear her out and get her really tired."

Tired could more likely be the word used to describe Faith since concerts often lasted until after 11:00 P.M. Yet Faith was committed to raising her daughters in person. "I'm a mother and a wife and just so happen to be an entertainer living out my lifelong dream. It's a constant job running here, there, picking up this and that, changing, feeding, and trying to entertain. This hurricane can be so exhausting."

The Soul2Soul Tour 2000 was a huge success with sold-out arenas in cities like Washington, DC, and Chicago. New York City's Madison Square Garden sold out of tickets to the show in less than two hours. In August, Faith picked up six award nominations from the Country Music Association: Female Vocalist of the Year, Album of the Year for *Breathe*, Vocal Event of the Year with Tim on "Let's Make Love," and Single and Music Video of the Year for "Breathe." Faith was also nominated for the coveted Entertainer of the Year Award.

Tim also was nominated for several awards, including Entertainer of the Year. The couple joked about keeping the award in the family one way or another, and Faith voiced her surprise at the multiple nominations. "This is just

incredible. I am overwhelmed. I am so grateful to all who nominated me."

Another honor was given to Faith when she was chosen to open the televised October 5th awards show. That night, the television camera zoomed through Nashville's evening sky before focusing on the brightly lit Grand Ole Opry House. The next shot showed the stage inside the Opry House as the Country Music Association began its 34th annual awards show.

The Opry stage was black and white as white spotlights bounced from above onto stark black scaffolding. Into this scene walked Faith, wearing a black pants suit. Her band was dressed in black as well and stood or sat on the scaffolding

Faith and Tim embarked on their Soul2Soul Tour 2000 on July 12th of that year. Faith also recorded the song, "Where Are You Christmas," for Jim Carrey's movie, *Dr. Suess' How the Grinch Stole Christmas*.

At the 2000 Country Music Awards, Faith Hill won awards for Top Female Artist and Video of the Year for "Let's Make Love."

behind her. As a thin cloud of stage smoke rose around her knees, she began singing "There Will Come a Day."

Faith acknowledged the enthusiastic response from her audience with a bow, and then she sat next to Tim in the audience to watch the rest of the ceremony. By the end of the show, Tim and Faith had been awarded matching statuettes for Male Vocalist of the Year and Female Vocalist of the Year. The coveted Entertainer of the Year award went to the Dixie Chicks.

In November, Faith recorded a musical number that was sure to please Gracie and Maggie. She sang "Where Are You Christmas," which was included in the hit Universal Pictures movie, *Dr. Suess' How the Grinch Stole Christmas*, starring Jim Carrey.

When the Soul2Soul Tour 2000 finally ended in December, it stood as the highest-grossing country tour of the year, with total gross proceeds of more than $45 million. Over 1 million fans had seen the concert.

Faith's Thanksgiving evening television special was taped ahead of time so she was able to spend the holiday with her family. She certainly could have been giving thanks for an enormously successful year in terms of her career, but it's more likely she was giving thanks for her husband, daughters, family, and good friends.

During the summer of 2000, Faith talked about the important things in her life. "I want to be a great mother. I want to teach my children to really appreciate the simple things in life. And I am learning as I go. My mother and father gave me love; they gave all of us love. And they listened to us. That's the way I want to be."

CHRONOLOGY

1967   Born on September 21 in Jackson, Mississippi, and adopted by Ted and Edna Perry.

1974   First public performance at a 4-H mother-daughter luncheon.

1986   Graduated from McLaurin High School, Star, Mississippi.

1987   Moved to Nashville, Tennessee, to break into music business.

1988   Married Daniel Hill.

1991   Signed recording contract with Warner Brothers Records.

1993   *Take Me as I Am* is released.

1994   Single "Wild One" is number one on *Billboard* chart for four weeks; divorced from Daniel Hill; undergoes successful throat surgery.

1995   Becomes engaged to Scott Hendricks; *It Matters to Me* is released.

1996   Single "It Matters to Me" is number one for three weeks; embarks on the Spontaneous Combustion Tour; marries Tim McGraw.

1997   Daughter Gracie is born on May 5; single "This Kiss" hits top five on pop charts.

1998   Daughter Maggie is born on August 12; third album, *Faith*, is released.

1999   "This Kiss" tour is Faith's first headlining tour; appears on *Divas Live;* single "Breathe" hits number one on both pop and country charts

2000   Embarks on the Soul2Soul Tour 2000 with Tim; Faith hosts a Thanksgiving television special.

ACCOMPLISHMENTS

Albums

1993 *Take Me as I Am*

1995 *It Matters to Me*

1998 *Faith*

1999 *Breathe*

Singles

1993 *Wild One*

1994 *Piece of My Heart*
But I Will

1995 *Let's Go to Vegas*
It Matters to Me

1998 *This Kiss*

2000 *The Way You Love Me*
Breathe

Awards

1993 Country Music Association (CMA) Top New Female Vocalist

1994 Billboard Top Female Country Artist
Performance Magazine Best Female Country Artist

1995 TNN/Music City News Award Star of Tomorrow Award

1997 (CMA) Vocal Event of the Year for "It's Your Love" duet with Tim McGraw
Academy of Country Music (ACM) Vocal Event of the Year for "It's Your Love"
(ACM) Video of the Year for "It's Your Love"
(ACM) Song of the Year for "It's Your Love"
(ACM) Single of the Year for "It's Your Love"

1998 (ACM) Vocal Event of the Year for "Just to Hear You Say That You Love Me" duet with Tim McGraw
(ACM) Top Female Vocalist
(ACM) Video of the Year for "This Kiss"
(ACM) Single of the Year for "This Kiss"

1999 (CMA) Song of the Year
(ACM) Top Female Vocalist
(ACM) Video of the Year for "Breath"

2000 (CMA) Female Vocalist of the Year
(ACM) Top Female Vocalist

FURTHER READING

Gray, Scott. *Perfect Harmony: The Faith Hill and Tim McGraw Story.* New York: Ballantine Books, 1999.

Kingsbury, Paul. *The Grand Ole Opry History of Country Music.* New York: Random House, 1995.

Oermann, Robert. *A Century of Country: An Illustrated History of Country Music.* TV Books Inc., 1999.

Paterson, Katherine. *Come Sing, Jimmy Jo.* New York: Putnam Books for Young Readers, 1994.

Zymet, Cathy Alter. *LeAnn Rimes.* Philadelphia: Chelsea House Publishers, 1999.

Website
www.faithhill.com

ABOUT THE AUTHOR

Southwest Missouri writer BONNIE HINMAN has had five children's historical novels and two children's biographies published, as well as many articles and stories. She enjoys speaking at schools and reading all kinds of books. Mrs. Hinman lives with her husband, Bill, and son Brad in Joplin, Missouri, where her daughter Beth and son-in-law Eric also reside.

INDEX

America's Promise, 47

Big Oak Ranch, 54-55

Borman, Gary, 24, 27

Brandy, 44

Breathe (album), 49, 51-52, 56

"Breathe" (song), 8, 51, 52, 56

Brooks & Dunn, 28

Burr, Gary, 23

Chase, David, 20-21

Cher, 44

Chesney, Kenny, 54

Cover Girl Cosmetics, 44-46

Denton, Keith, 54

Divas Live (TV), 44

Divas 2000: A Tribute to Diana Ross (TV), 52

Dixie Chicks, 58

Faith (album), 42-43

Faith Hill Family Literacy Project, 36, 47

Gary Morris Music, 19, 20, 21

Grand Ole Opry, 11-12, 20, 25, 57

Grant, Amy, 43

Hay, George, 11

Hendricks, Scott, 23, 30, 33, 36

Hill, Daniel (first husband), 19-20, 24-25

Hill, Faith

  adoption, 15, 24, 25

  albums, 25-27, 28, 30-31, 33-34, 42-43, 44, 47, 49, 51-52, 56, 58

  awards, 28, 42, 47, 54, 56, 58

birth, 15

childhood, 15-18

as commercial spokesperson, 44-46

divorce, 24-25

early career, 18-25

education, 16, 17, 18

and literacy, 16, 36, 47

marriages, 19, 37-38

and television, 7-9, 25, 27, 44, 52, 59

and throat surgery, 28-29, 30

Houston, Whitney, 44, 52

How the Grinch Stole Christmas, 59

It Matters to Me (album), 30-31, 33-34

"It Matters to Me" (song), 8, 34

"It Scares Me" (song), 21

"It's Your Love" (song), 39, 42

Jackson, Alan, 28, 34

Jones, Cathy, 17

"Keep Walkin' On" (song), 33-34

"Let's Go to Vegas" (song), 33

"Let's Make Love" (song), 8, 51, 56

Lynne, Shelby, 34

McEntire, Reba, 13, 17, 18-19, 27-28

McGraw, Tim (second husband), 7-8, 34-36, 37-38, 42, 43, 46-47, 51, 52-55, 56, 58, 59

McGraw, Gracie Katherine (daughter), 41-42, 43, 46-47, 55-56, 58, 59

McGraw, Maggie Elizabeth (daughter), 44, 46-47, 55-56, 58, 59

"Man's Home is His Castle, A" (song), 33

Montgomery, John Michael, 28

Nashville Now (TV), 25

Perry, Edna (mother), 15, 16, 18, 24, 25, 28

Perry, Steve (brother), 15-16

Perry, Ted (father), 15, 16, 18, 24, 25

Perry, Wesley (brother), 15-16, 24

"Piece of My Heart" (song), 27

Powell, Colin, 47

Presley, Elvis, 12, 16-17

Sharp, Martha, 23-24

Star, Mississippi, 15

Strait, George, 13, 43, 54

Summer Olympics, 1996, 36-37

Super Bowl XXXIV, 52

Take Me as I Am (album), 15-27

Thanksgiving television special, 7-9, 59

"There Will Come A Day" (song), 8, 58

"This Kiss" (song), 7, 43-44, 46, 47, 49

Trimble, Betty, 35, 37

Turner, Tina, 44

Warner Brothers Records, 23, 27, 36

"Where Are You Christmas" (song), 58-59

"Wild One" (song), 26-27